SNAP
REVISION

GENES, INHERITANCE AND SELECTION & GLOBAL CHALLENGES

OCR Gateway GCSE Biology

OCR
GATEWAY
GCSE
BIOLOGY

REVISE TRICKY TOPICS IN A SNAP

Contents

Published by Collins
An imprint of HarperCollinsPublishers
1 London Bridge Street,
London, SE1 9GF

© HarperCollinsPublishers Limited 2016

9780008218102

First published 2016

10 9 8 7 6 5 4 3 2 1

British Library Cataloguing in Publication Data.

A CIP record of this book is available from the British Library.

Printed in United Kingdom by Martins the Printers

ACKNOWLEDGEMENTS

The author and publisher are grateful to the copyright holders for permission to use quoted materials and images.

p21 MARGRIT HIRSCH/Shutterstock.com; p29 Holly Kuchera/Shutterstock.com; p29 elbud/Shutterstock.com; p29 Denis Pepin/Shutterstock.com

Every effort has been made to trace copyright holders and obtain their permission for the use of copyright material. The author and publisher will gladly receive information enabling them to rectify any error or omission in subsequent editions. All facts are correct at time of going to press.

HT Higher Tier content

How To Use This Book

To get the most out of this revision guide, just work your way through the book in the order it is presented.

This is how it works:

Revise
Clear and concise revision notes help you get to grips with the topic

Revise
Key Points and Key Words explain the important information you need to know

Revise
A Quick Test at the end of every topic is a great way to check your understanding

Practise
Practice questions for each topic reinforce the revision content you have covered

Review
The Review section is a chance to revisit the topic to improve your recall in the exam

Genes

You must be able to:

- Explain the relationship between genes, chromosomes and the genome
- Describe how genes and the environment influence phenotype
- Recall that genetic variants may or may not influence phenotype
- HT Describe how genetic variants may influence phenotype.

Genes and Chromosomes

- Chromosomes are made of DNA and are found inside the nucleus.
- Each chromosome contains a number of genes.
- A gene is section of DNA that codes for a protein.
- A genome is an organism's complete set of DNA, including all of its genes.

Genotype and Phenotype

- Genes are responsible for our characteristics.
- We have two copies of every chromosome in our cells, therefore, we have two copies of each gene.
- The different forms of each gene are called alleles.
- We use capital and lower case letters to show if alleles are dominant or recessive.
- If two dominant alleles are present, e.g. BB, the dominant characteristic is seen, e.g. brown eyes.
- If two recessive alleles are present, e.g. bb, the recessive characteristic is seen, e.g. blue eyes.
- If one of each allele is present, e.g. Bb, the dominant character is seen, e.g. brown eyes.
- In the case of eye colour for example, brown eyes are dominant and would be shown as BB or Bb.
- Blue eyes on the other hand, are recessive and would be shown as bb.
- The phenotype is the characteristic that is seen, e.g. blue eyes.
- The genotype is the genes that are present, e.g. bb.

A Cell

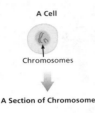

Chromosomes

A Section of Chromosome

← A gene

A Section of DNA

A Section of Uncoiled DNA

	A person who is heterozygous has two different alleles.	A person who is homozygous has both alleles the same.
Genes on Chromosomes		
Alleles	One allele for blue eyes, one for brown eyes	Both alleles are for blue eyes
Heterozygous or Homozygous	Heterozygous	Homozygous
Genotype	Bb	bb
Phenotype	Brown eyes	Blue eyes

> **Key Point**
>
> Capital letters represent dominant alleles.
>
> Lower case letters represent recessive alleles.

> **Key Point**
>
> A human body cell has 46 chromosomes, arranged in 23 pairs.

Environment and Phenotype

- Inherited variation is caused by the genes inherited from parents.
- Environmental variation is caused by environmental factors, e.g. diet.
- The phenotype of an organism is often the result of both genetic and environmental variation.
- For example:
  - a person who inherits light skin may, through prolonged exposure to the sun, develop darker skin
  - a person who inherits 'tall' genes may not grow tall if poorly nourished.
- Some characteristics show continuous variation, for example height. A person can be tall or short or anywhere in between the two.
- Characteristics that show discontinuous variation have a limited number of possible values. For example, blood groups are either A, B, AB or O.

Characteristics Controlled Solely by Inheritance	Factors that are Influenced by Environment and Inheritance
Eye colour	Height and weight
Hair colour	Intelligence
Blood group	Artistic or sporting ability
Inherited diseases	Skin colour

Mutations and Phenotype

- Sometimes, when DNA is copied, it results in a mutation or genetic variant. Often this mutation has no effect on phenotype.

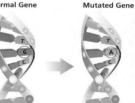

Normal Gene   Mutated Gene

The G base is substituted for an A base

HT If the mutation happens in coding DNA, it can affect the structure of proteins made.

HT The protein may:
  - continue to function normally
  - have reduced function
  - lose its function completely.

HT In enzymes, the active site may no longer fit the substrate.

HT In humans, about 98% of DNA does not code for protein production.

HT Some of this DNA controls whether a gene is expressed by turning gene transcription on or off.

HT If a mutation happens in non-coding DNA it may alter how genes are expressed.

Key Words

chromosome
DNA
gene
genome
allele
dominant
recessive
phenotype
genotype
heterozygous
homozygous
continuous
discontinuous
variant

Quick Test

1. What is a genome?
2. How do we show whether an allele is dominant or recessive?
3. Suggest two characteristics that may be affected by the environment.
4. Give an example of:
   a) continuous variation   b) discontinuous variation.

Genetics and Reproduction

You must be able to:

- Explain advantages and disadvantages of sexual and asexual reproduction
- Describe meiosis and explain its role in genetic variation
- Use genetic crosses to determine the outcomes for sex and other characteristics
- Describe the work of Mendel in developing our understanding of genetics.

Sexual and Asexual Reproduction

Type of Reproduction / Features	Sexual	Asexual
Gametes (sex cells)	Involves fusion of two gametes	Gametes not involved
Parents	Two parents	One parent
Variation	Produces variation in offspring (this is important in the process of natural selection)	No variation – offspring are clones of parent (a possible disadvantage since the whole population could be susceptible to an environmental pressure)
Where it is found	Method of reproduction in most animals and plants	Bacteria, some plants and a small number of animals, e.g. starfish
Numbers of offspring	Number limited per birth	Can produce many offspring rapidly, which is an advantage

Meiosis

- Meiosis is a type of cell division that produces gametes.
- The cell divides twice to produce four gametes with genetically different sets of chromosomes.
- Gametes have half the number of chromosomes as body cells. This is called a haploid number.

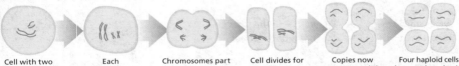

| Cell with two pairs of chromosomes (diploid cell). | Each chromosome replicates itself. | Chromosomes part company and move to opposite poles. | Cell divides for the first time. | Copies now separate and the second cell division takes place. | Four haploid cells (gametes), each with half the number of chromosomes of the parent cell. |

- When the gametes fuse in fertilisation, the normal diploid number of chromosomes is restored.
- Fusion of gametes is a source of genetic variation.

Determination of Sex

- Sex inheritance is controlled by a whole chromosome rather than a gene.
- In humans, the 23rd pair of chromosomes in males contains an X and a Y chromosome; females have two X chromosomes.

Key Point

The chance of having a male child is always 50%, as is the chance of having a female child.

Genetic Crosses

- A genetic cross looks at the possible outcomes for offspring with parents of the same or different genotypes.
- All the offspring of a cross between a homozygous dominant and a homozygous recessive will appear to have the dominant characteristic.
- A cross between two heterozygous parents will give a ratio of three offspring with the dominant characteristic to one with the recessive.

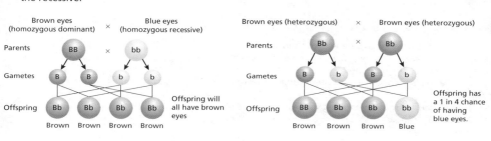

The Work of Mendel

- Gregor Mendel was a monk who spent many years researching inheritance in pea plants.
- He found that flowers were either purple or white with no intermediate colours.
- This challenged the hypotheses of other scientists who thought that inherited traits blend from one generation to the next.
- By doing thousands of experiments on pea plants, Mendel came up with three important conclusions:
  - Inheritance is determined by 'units'.
  - An individual inherits one 'unit' from each parent for each trait.
  - A trait may not show up in an individual but can be passed on.
- Mendel's 'units' are what we now know as genes.
- The principles he discovered for plants are essentially the same for most living things.

Key Point

Most of the characteristics we exhibit are not controlled by a single gene, but are the result of multiple gene inheritance.

Key Point

Scientists come up with a hypothesis and gather evidence. If the evidence supports the hypothesis, it is accepted until someone offers a better hypothesis and new evidence.

Quick Test

1. What is the difference between a haploid cell and a diploid cell? Give an example of each.
2. Give **three** differences between sexual and asexual reproduction.
3. Explain why there is a 50/50 chance of having a male or female baby.

Key Words

gamete
haploid
diploid

Natural Selection and Evolution

You must be able to:

- Understand there is extensive genetic variation within a population and relate this to evolution
- Describe the evidence for evolution and the work of Darwin and Wallace
- Explain how the development of ideas on evolution have impacted on modern biology, including the impact on classification systems.

Darwin's Theory of Evolution

- Evolution is the gradual change in the inherited characteristics of a population over a large number of generations, which may result in the formation of a new species.
- Charles Darwin's theory of evolution through natural selection suggested:
  - There is much variation within a species.
  - There is a struggle for survival and organisms have more offspring than can survive.
  - Those that are best adapted to their environment are likely to survive, breed and pass on their genes to the next generation (survival of the fittest).
  - Those that are least well adapted are likely to die.
- Another scientist called Alfred Wallace carried out similar research at the same time and supported Darwin's ideas about evolution.
- Darwin's theory was not accepted until after his death because there was not enough evidence (genes and the mechanism of inheritance had not been discovered).
- His ideas were not popular at the time because they contradicted the belief that God had created all life on Earth.
- There is still some debate among scientists today about how life began.
- The work of Darwin and Wallace had a profound impact on society at the time and continues to shape scientific understanding.
- At the time it created great controversy, but it also created a new line of thought.

Mutations

- Variation can arise because of mutations in a gene.
- If the mutation results in a characteristic that gives the organism an advantage over organisms without the characteristic, it is more likely to survive, breed and pass on the mutated gene to its offspring.

Using Darwin's idea of survival of the fittest, you might hypothesise:

'Animals that are better camouflaged are less likely to be seen by predators.'

A model can be used to test this hypothesis using blue, green, red and brown strands of wool:

Key Point

Scientific models are used to explain and predict the behaviour of real objects or systems that are difficult to observe directly.

- Thirty 5cm strands of each colour of wool are scattered randomly in a field.
- A group of students are given 1 minute to find as many strands as they can.

Using the model, you might predict that:

- More red and blue strands of wool will be found because they are not camouflaged.
- Fewer green and brown strands will be found because they are better camouflaged.

Evidence for Evolution

- The fossil record gives us evidence of change over a long period of time, however there are gaps in this record.
- Antibiotic resistance provides evidence for evolution – bacteria divide very rapidly, so evolution by natural selection can be seen in a very short period of time:
  - A mutation may cause a bacterium to be resistant to an antibiotic.
  - Most of the bacteria in the population are killed by the antibiotic.
  - The antibiotic-resistant bacteria multiply rapidly to form a colony of resistant bacteria.

Developments in Classification Systems

- Developments in biology have had a significant impact on classification systems.
- The binomial classification system places organisms into groups based on a large number of characteristics such as anatomy, physiology, biochemistry and reproduction.
- This helps us to understand how organisms are related to each other.
- Darwin's theory of evolution provided a new explanation for how to group organisms:
  - nearness of descent
  - phylogeny (the sequence of events involved in the evolution of a species).
- Phylogenetic systems of classification help us understand the evolutionary history of organisms:
  - DNA sequencing can be used to show if organisms share common ancestors.
  - DNA sequencing has led to some organisms being reclassified.

Natural Classification of Sumatran Orang-utan

Level	Example
Kingdom	Animalia
Phylum	Chordata
Class	Mammalia
Order	Primates
Family	Hominidae
Genus	*Pongo*
Species	*Pongo abelii*

The Bornean orang-utan, *Pongo pygmaeus*, shares the same genus, which shows they are closely related. They developed as two separate species following the separation of Borneo and Sumatra.

Phylogenetic Tree

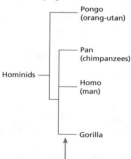

Pongo (orang-utan)

Pan (chimpanzees)

Hominids

Homo (man)

Gorilla

This shows that man, chimps, gorillas and orang-utans all share a common ancestor. It is thought that man is more closely related to gorillas than orang-utans.

1. Explain Darwin's theory of natural selection.
2. Explain how antibiotic resistance develops.
3. How does DNA sequencing help to classify organisms?

mutation
antibiotic resistance
phylogenetic

Genes

1 Put the following structures in order of size, starting with largest.

nucleus   gene   cell   chromosome   [1]

2 Inherited variation is caused by the genes inherited from parents.

Which of the following characteristics are solely due to inheritance?

A Blood group
B Shape of nose
C Height
D Eye colour   [2]

3 The diagram below shows the pairs of alleles for genes that code for tongue rolling, eye colour and attached earlobes.

Use the diagram to answer the following questions.

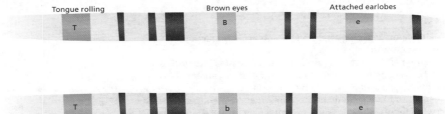

Tongue rolling   Brown eyes   Attached earlobes

Tongue rolling   Blue eyes   Attached earlobes

a) Is tongue rolling dominant or recessive?   [1]

b) Is the individual homozygous or heterozygous for eye colour?   [1]

c) What is the genotype for attached earlobes?   [1]

4 HT Changes in gene expression can result from changes in the DNA sequence.

Which type of DNA will be affected by these changes?   [1]

Total Marks _____ / 7

Genetics and Reproduction

1 Fill in the spaces on the diagram below to show how many chromosomes are present in each of these human cells.

Sperm   **Egg**   **Fertilised Egg Cell**

 + =

_____   _____   _____

[3]

2 For each of the statements below, decide if they best describe **sexual** or **asexual** reproduction:

a) Involves two parents [1]

b) The offspring are genetically different from parents [1]

c) No gametes involved [1]

d) Provides variation [1]

e) Only one parent [1]

f) Offspring are clones of parent [1]

g) Limited number of offspring produced [1]

3 In meiosis, how many gametes are produced from one parent cell? [1]

4 The diagram below shows the chromosomes from a human body cell.

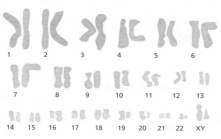

a) Does this cell come from a male or female? [1]

b) Is the cell haploid or diploid? [1]

c) A meerkat egg cell has 18 chromosomes. How many chromosomes in a meerkat body cell? [1]

Practice Questions

5. Cystic fibrosis in an inherited disease caused by a recessive gene.
People who have one dominant and one recessive allele are known as carriers.
People who have two recessive alleles will have cystic fibrosis.

The diagram below shows a cross between two carriers of cystic fibrosis.

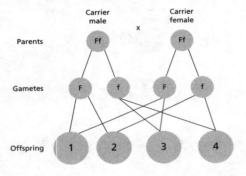

a) For each of the offspring, 1–4, write their genotype. [4]

b) What are the numbers of the offspring who will be carriers? [2]

c) Which number offspring will have the disease? [1]

Total Marks _____ / 21

Natural Selection and Evolution

1. Charles Darwin published his theory of evolution at a time when genes had yet to be discovered. His theory was based on the idea of natural selection.

a) What is meant by natural selection? [1]

b) Evolution is a slow process but can be seen quickly when bacteria develop antibiotic resistance.

Explain how antibiotic resistance develops. [3]

2   The diagram below shows a phylogenetic tree.

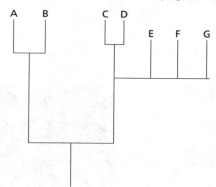

Use the diagram to decide which pair of organisms is most closely related in each question below.

a) Organisms **C** and **D** or Organisms **B** and **C**?   [1]

b) Organisms **E** and **F** or Organisms **D** and **E**?   [1]

c) Organisms **C** and **G** or Organisms **A** and **G**?   [1]

Total Marks _____ / 7

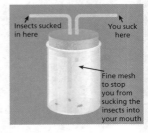

Monitoring and Maintaining the Environment

You must be able to:

- Explain how to carry out field investigations into the distribution and abundance of organisms in a habitat
- Describe how human interactions affect ecosystems
- Explain the benefits and challenges of maintaining biodiversity
- **HT** Evaluate evidence for impact of environmental changes.

Distribution and Abundance

- Scientists studying the environment often want to investigate:
  - the distribution of an organism (where it is found)
  - the numbers of organisms in a given area or habitat.
- The following apparatus can be used for sampling:

Apparatus	What it is Used For
Pooter	Catching small insects on the ground
Pitfall traps	Catching small crawling insects
Pond net	Catching water invertebrates, small fish
Sweep net	Catching flying insects
Quadrat	Sampling the number of plant species
Line transects	Sampling the distribution of plant species

- A key can be used to identify the organisms found.

A Quadrat

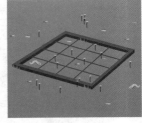

A Sweep Net

A Pitfall Trap

A Pooter

Insects sucked in here You suck here

Fine mesh to stop you from sucking the insects into your mouth

The Capture–Mark–Recapture Method

- Follow the steps below to estimate the number of animals in an area using the capture–mark–recapture method:
  1. Count the animals caught in the trap.
  2. Mark them and release them.
  3. Count the animals caught a few days later, noting how many are marked / not marked.

$$\text{population size} = \frac{\text{number in 1st sample} \times \text{number in 2nd sample}}{\text{number in 2nd sample that are marked}}$$

Using Quadrats

- Follow the steps below to estimate the number of plants in a field:
  1. Measure the area of the field.
  2. Randomly place a number of quadrats (1 square metre) in the field.
  3. Count the number of plants in each quadrat.
  4. Work out the mean number of plants per quadrat.
  5. Multiply by the number of square metres in the field.

Human Interactions and Ecosystems

- Humans need to obtain and produce resources to survive.
- Their interactions have a huge impact on ecosystems.
- Deforestation, hunting and pesticides impact negatively on ecosystems.
- To prevent further damage to ecosystems, conservation methods are employed.
- Captive breeding programmes, creating nature reserves, sustainable fishing and passing laws to protect animals have a positive impact on ecosystems.
- Ecotourism aims to reduce the impact of tourism on environments by not interfering with wildlife, leaving a low carbon footprint and supporting the local community. It is an example of sustainable development.

> **Key Point**
>
> Activities such as farming, fishing, hunting and building can often have a negative impact on ecosystems.

Biodiversity

- The greater the biodiversity, the greater the stability of an ecosystem and the greater the opportunity for medical discoveries.
- Biodiversity boosts the economy, e.g. a greater variety of plants means a greater variety of crops.
- The challenges of maintaining diversity arise due to:
  - **Political issues** – conservation strategies are often politically sensitive and there may be difficulty in gaining agreements between local, national and global partners.
  - **Economic issues** – conservation is often expensive, for example, trying to monitor conservation schemes.

HT Impact of Environmental Changes

- Evidence suggests that rising levels of greenhouse gases have led to a rise in global temperatures, which melts polar ice caps and causes sea levels to rise.
- Rising temperatures also cause changes to distributions of organisms, e.g. some animal and plant species have moved further north or to higher, cooler areas and some birds are migrating earlier.

> **Quick Test**
>
> 1. Why is biodiversity important?
> 2. Suggest **two** ways in which human activity impacts:
>   a) negatively on biodiversity
>   b) positively on biodiversity.
> 3. What is ecotourism?

> **Key Words**
>
> habitat
> sustainable
> ecotourism
> biodiversity

Investigations

You must be able to:

- Explain how to determine the number of organisms in a given area
- Plan and explain investigations
- Select appropriate apparatus and recognise when to apply sampling techniques
- Translate data and carry out statistical analysis, identifying potential sources of error
- Recognise the importance of peer review of results.

Planning and Carrying Out Investigations

- When planning an investigation many factors must be considered and certain steps should always be followed.

At the edge of the school field are some large trees that shade part of the field for much of the day.

A group of students wanted to find out if the shade from the trees affected the number of dandelions growing in the field.

Investigation:
How is the distribution of dandelions affected by light and shade?

> The rationale for the investigation can be incorporated into the title.

Hypothesis:
There will be more dandelions growing the further you get from the trees because there will be more light.

> The hypothesis should always be based on scientific knowledge.

Method:

1. Measure a transect from the trees to the edge of the field.
2. At 5-metre intervals along the transect, place a quadrat on the ground.

> Apparatus should always be appropriate, e.g. you would not use a ruler to measure 5-metre intervals.

3. Count the number of dandelions in each quadrat.

> Scientists use sampling and look at several small areas to get a good representation of the whole area.

4. Carry out two more transects, parallel to the first one, and count the dandelions in each quadrat. This will improve the reliability of the results.
5. Work out the average number of dandelions at each distance from the trees.

> Any data recorded should be reliable, which means readings should be repeated.

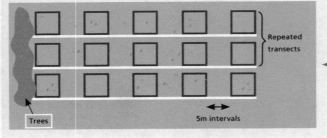

Repeated transects

5m intervals

Trees

> A diagram often helps to clarify the method.

Results:

Distance from Trees (m)	0	5	10	15	20
Number of Dandelions in each Transect	8	9	7	6	5
	8	8	7	2	6
	9	6	5	6	4
Mean Number	8.3	7	6.3	4.7	5.0

Data needs to be presented in an organised way, e.g. tables are useful for presenting data clearly.

Data sometimes needs to be analysed statistically by calculating the mean, mode or median.

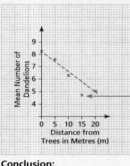

Line graphs are often useful for spotting anomalous results, which are often due to human errors, e.g. misreading the tape measure, or may occur randomly by chance.

Conclusion:

* The results show that the further you go from the trees, the fewer dandelions are growing, i.e. the opposite of what was predicted.

Evaluation:

* It was difficult to control variables such as the moisture content of the soil and the ground temperature, which could have affected the number of dandelions.
* To improve the experiment, a digital light meter could have been used to give some light readings for each quadrat.
* The experiment could be repeated at a different time of the year.

The evaluation should consider the method and results and what improvements could be made.

If the conclusion is different to what was predicted, the question 'why' must be asked and this may generate a new hypothesis, which can then be tested.

Key Point

Systemic / systematic errors occur when the same error is made every time. Systematic errors are only likely to be discovered if someone else tries to repeat the experiment and does not achieve the same results.

Key Point

A **peer review** is when one scientist evaluates another's experiment. This is valuable for scrutinising the design of the experiment and the validity of the data, and providing credibility.

Key Words

rationale
hypothesis
sampling
reliable
anomalous
systemic / systematic error
peer review

Quick Test

1. How do you ensure results from an investigation are reliable?
2. What is an anomalous result?
3. What are systemic / systematic errors?
4. Why is peer review important?

Feeding the Human Race

You must be able to:

- Describe biological factors affecting food security
- Describe how agriculture and farming are attempting to meet the growing demands for food
- Describe the process of genetic engineering and the benefits and risks of using gene technology in food production
- Explain how biotechnology can help in food production.

Food Security

- Factors that affect food security include:
  - the continually increasing global population, which requires more food to be produced
  - demand for a wider variety of food in wealthier populations
  - the appearance of new pests and pathogens, which can harm food supplies
  - environmental changes, such as global warming
  - the high cost of modern farming methods
  - sustainable developments, which limit food resources.

> **Key Point**
>
> Food security is all people having access to sufficient, safe, nutritious food.

Agricultural Solutions

Hydroponics	Biological Control
Hydroponics involves growing plants in nutrient solutions instead of soil. Plants can be grown at all times of the year providing the environment is controlled. Correct mineral levels can be easily provided.	Biological control is an environmentally friendly way of controlling pests. Organisms that feed on the pest (a predator species) are released into the crop, e.g. using ladybirds to reduce the number of greenfly.
Gene Technology	**Fertilisers and Pesticides**
Genetically modified (GM) plants have had genes added, which give them desirable traits, e.g. drought or pest resistance.	Fertilisers supply plants with all the nutrients they need to grow quickly and healthily. Pesticides are chemicals sprayed onto plants to kill animal and plant pests that might harm plant growth.

Selective Breeding

- Selective breeding is the process of finding plants or animals with the best characteristics and breeding them.
- The process is repeated many times until the desired characteristic is present in all offspring.
- Selective breeding has been used to produce:
  - disease-resistant wheat
  - dairy cattle that give high milk yields
  - wheat that grows in areas of high salt levels.

Hydroponics

Fertilisers and Pesticides

Genetic Engineering

- Genetic engineering involves altering the genome of an organism by adding a gene, or genes, from a different organism.
- It uses enzymes to 'cut and paste' genes.

Benefits of GM Foods	Risks of GM Foods
Higher crop yields	Once out in the wild it is impossible to recall genetically modified organisms
More nutritious crops	Genetically modified organisms may breed with other non-GM organisms passing on these new foreign genes into the wild population, for example, spread of herbicide-resistant genes might lead to super weeds
Crops can grow in harsh environments	We do not know the long-term effects of eating GM food; GM foods may harm the consumer, for example, causing allergic reactions
Crops resistant to pests and disease	
Better flavour food	
Food with longer shelf life	

HT The process of genetic engineering:

Steps of Genetic Engineering

1. A strand of DNA is taken from the organism that has the useful characteristic.
2. The gene for the useful characteristic is isolated and cut from the DNA using restriction enzymes. Some enzymes produce DNA with short, single-stranded pieces at the ends – these are called sticky ends.
3. The desired gene is 'pasted' into the DNA of the organism that requires the useful characteristic using ligase enzymes.

1 Desired gene

2 Desired gene isolated

3 Desired gene inserted into DNA of a different organism

HT A plasmid vector is a small loop of DNA often containing 'marker' genes for antibiotic resistance:
- Protein-making genes can be inserted into plasmids.
- The plasmids are mixed with bacteria.
- Only the bacteria that take up the plasmid will grow on medium containing antibiotics, due to the marker genes.
- These host bacteria are encouraged to multiply, producing large amounts of the desired protein.

Biotechnology and Food Production

- Microorganisms (bacteria and fungi) can be grown in fermenters on a large scale to produce foods such as mycoprotein and yoghurt.

Key Words

selective breeding
HT restriction enzymes
HT ligase enzymes
HT plasmid
HT vector
HT host bacteria
fermenter
mycoprotein

Quick Test

1. What is food security?
2. What is biological control?
3. Explain the risks associated with GM crops.

Monitoring and Maintaining Health

You must be able to:

- Describe different types of diseases
- Describe how diseases spread and how this spread may be reduced
- Describe defence responses in animals and plants to disease
- **HT** Describe how plant diseases can be detected and identified
- Explain how white blood cells and platelets are adapted to their function.

Diseases

- Communicable diseases are easily transmitted.
- They are caused by bacteria, viruses, fungi, protoctista or parasites.
- Sometimes diseases interact with each other, for example:
  - People with HIV (human immunodeficiency virus) are more likely to catch tuberculosis (TB) than those without HIV because of a weakened immune system.
  - Infection with some types of human papillomavirus can lead to the development of cervical cancer.

Spread of Disease

- Communicable diseases can be spread in humans in a number of ways, as shown in the table below:

Method of Spread	Examples
In the air through droplets, when people sneeze or cough	Chicken pox, tuberculosis, colds
By eating contaminated food	*Salmonella* food poisoning
By drinking contaminated water	Cholera
Contact – person to person or person to object	Athlete's foot
Animals – through bites or scratches	Malaria

- Spread of disease in humans can be reduced by good hygiene:
  - handle and prepare food safely
  - wash hands frequently
  - sneeze into a tissue then bin it
  - do not share personal items, e.g. a toothbrush
  - get vaccinated
  - do not touch wild animals.
- Communicable diseases can spread rapidly and infect millions of people globally.
- Statistics on the incidence and spread of communicable diseases are collected by Communicable Disease Centres.

Key Point

Health is more than just the absence of disease. It is defined as a state of complete physical, mental and social wellbeing.

Key Point

HIV is the virus that causes AIDS. It is possible to have the virus but not have AIDS. The virus is usually sexually transmitted and attacks the immune system making sufferers vulnerable to infection. There is no cure, but there are treatments to help manage the disease.

Key Point

Scientific quantities (i.e. statistics) allow us to predict likely trends in the number of cases of diseases and how the disease will spread nationally and globally. This is very important when planning for a country's future health needs.

Plants and Disease

- Plant diseases are caused by bacteria, viruses or fungi, and are spread by contact, insects, wind or water.
- Plants have cell walls and waxy epidermal cuticles, which form a barrier against plant pathogens.
- Plants can also produce toxic chemicals and pathogen-degrading enzymes as a response to infection.
- Spread of disease in plants can be reduced by:
  - using insecticides to kill pests which may carry disease
  - allowing space between plants
  - crop rotation
  - spraying crops with fungicide or bactericide.

HT Plant diseases can be detected:
  - in the laboratory, by analysing DNA to see if it contains DNA or antigens from the infecting organisms
  - in the field by observation and microscopy.

Pear Rust Caused by a Fungus

Other examples of plant diseases include: virus tobacco mosaic virus (TMV), fungal Erysiphe graminis (barley powdery mildew) and crown gall disease.

Human Defences to Disease

- Human's first line of defence is to stop microorganisms entering the body:
  - the skin acts as a physical barrier
  - platelets help the blood to clot and seal wounds to prevent pathogens entering
  - mucous membranes in the lungs produce mucus, which traps microorganisms
  - acid in the stomach kills microorganisms in food.

White Blood Cells

- White blood cells engulf and destroy microbes by a process called phagocytosis.
- Some white blood cells, called B lymphocytes, also produce antibodies.
- The lymphocyte recognises antigens on the surface of the invading pathogen.
- It produces antibodies that lock onto the antigen.
- The antibodies are specific for that antigen.

Phagocytosis

White blood cell (phagocyte)

 Microorganisms invade the body.

 The white blood cell surrounds and ingests the microorganisms.

 The white blood cell starts to digest the microorganisms.

 The microorganisms have been digested by the white blood cell.

Antibody Production by White Blood Cells

Microorganisms (antigens) invade the body.

The white blood cell forms antibodies.

The antibodies cause the microorganisms to clump.

The white blood cell destroys the microorganisms.

Key Words

communicable
insecticide
fungicide
bactericide
platelets
phagocytosis
antibody
antigen

Quick Test

1. Name four groups of organism which cause disease.
2. Suggest three ways diseases can be spread in humans.
3. Suggest three ways to reduce the spread of disease in plants.

Prevention and Treatment of Disease

You must be able to:

- HT Describe how monoclonal antibodies are produced and how they can be used
- Explain the role of vaccination and medicines in the prevention and treatment of disease
- Explain aseptic techniques
- Describe the process of developing new medicines.

HT Monoclonal Antibodies

- Monoclonal antibodies are clones of antibodies made in the laboratory.
- B lymphocytes, which produce large amounts of antibody, are fused with tumour cells that divide quickly.
- The resulting hybridoma cells will divide quickly and produce lots of identical antibodies – monoclonal antibodies.
- The monoclonal antibodies will bind to the specific antigen to which the B lymphocytes have been exposed.

Production of Monoclonal Antibodies

Vaccinate mouse to stimulate the production of antibodies.

Collect spleen cells that form antibodies from mouse.

Tumour cells (myeloma)

Spleen and myeloma cells fuse to form hybridoma cells.

Grow hybridoma cells in tissue culture and select antibody-forming cells.

Collect monoclonal antibodies.

Pregnancy Tests	Diagnosing Cancer	Treating Cancer
Monoclonal antibodies can be made that bind to the hormone found in the urine of pregnant women.	Monoclonal antibodies can be produced that bind to cancer cells. The antibodies are labelled with a radioactive substance, making cancer cells easy to see on images taken with a special camera.	Drugs that treat cancer can be attached to monoclonal antibodies. The antibodies find and bind to cancer cells, delivering the drug to the cells.

Vaccination

- Vaccination (or immunisation) prevents people from getting a disease.
- The vaccine contains a dead or weakened version of the disease-causing organism.
- White blood cells (B lymphocytes) recognise the antigens present in the vaccine and produce antibodies.
- Memory cells are also produced that will recognise the disease-causing organism should the body come into contact with it again.
- If this happens, they will make lots of antibodies very quickly to prevent the person catching the disease.

- If a large percentage of the population have been vaccinated, only a small percentage of the population will be at risk from catching the disease and passing it on to others.
- Vaccination is important in controlling the spread of disease. Common childhood vaccinations include:
  - MMR (mumps, measles and rubella)
  - diptheria
  - tetanus.

Antibiotics, Antivirals and Antiseptics

- Antibiotics, e.g. penicillin, are used to treat bacterial infections.
- They cannot be used for viral infections because viruses are found inside cells and the antibiotic would damage the cell.
- Antivirals are drugs that treat viral infections.
- Antiseptics are chemicals that kill microorganisms outside the body. They can be used on skin, on surfaces and on wounds.

Aseptic Techniques

- When bacteria are grown in the laboratory it is important to use aseptic techniques.
- This minimises the risk of bacteria contaminating the surrounding area and also the chance of unwanted bacteria contaminating the cultures you are trying to grow.
- When working with cultures of bacteria:
  - use alcohol to clean the work surfaces
  - work in a small area surrounding a Bunsen burner flame
  - sterilise all glassware and media using an autoclave.

Developing New Medicines

- New medicines must be tested for toxicity, efficacy (effectiveness) and dosage before they are released to the public.
- There are a number of stages in developing a new drug:
  1. Tested on computer models or cells grown in the laboratory.
  2. Tested on animals, e.g. mice.
  3. Tested on small numbers of healthy volunteers in clinical trials (low doses often used).
  4. Further clinical trials on people with the disease, using control groups who are given a placebo.

> ## Key Point
>
> It is important to finish a course of antibiotics. Even when a person is feeling better, there are still infectious organisms in the body.

Sterilising an Inoculating Loop

Hold inoculating loop in Bunsen flame until red hot

Bunsen burner

Petri dish

Agar

Key Words

- HT clone
- HT hybridoma
- memory cells
- antibiotic
- antiviral
- antiseptic
- placebo

Quick Test

1. HT What is a hybridoma cell?
2. HT Give three uses of monoclonal antibodies.
3. How does vaccination work?
4. Distinguish between antibiotics, antivirals and antiseptics.

Non-Communicable Diseases

You must be able to:

- Recall some non-communicable diseases, suggest factors that contribute to them and evaluate data on them
- Evaluate some of the treatments for cardiovascular disease
- Discuss benefits and risks associated with using stem cells and gene technology in medicine
- Suggest why understanding the human genome is important in medicine.

Non-Communicable Diseases

- Many non-communicable diseases have contributory factors linked to lifestyle factors.
- Many of these factors interact with each other.
- For example, poor diet and lack of exercise can lead to obesity, which in turn is a risk factor for many diseases such as type 2 diabetes and cardiovascular disease.
- The arrows on the diagram below show the complex interaction of these factors.

> **Key Point**
>
> Cancer occurs when a cell mutates and begins to grow and divide uncontrollably. Such groups of cells are called tumours.

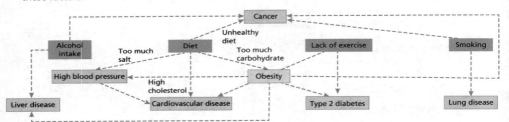

- Heart disease can be treated by:
  - **changes to lifestyle** – stopping smoking, eating healthily, exercising more
  - **medication** – there are a variety of medicines that can be taken to reduce high blood pressure, which is linked to heart disease, e.g. **statins** can be prescribed to lower cholesterol levels and aspirin can be taken to reduce the risk of further heart attacks
  - **surgery** – **stents** can be placed in narrowed arteries and heart transplants can replace damaged or diseased hearts.

> **Key Point**
>
> Cardiovascular disease is disease of the heart and / or blood vessels.

> **Key Point**
>
> You will often be asked to evaluate data to suggest the link between two variables.

Evaluating Data

- Smoking and lung cancer in the UK:

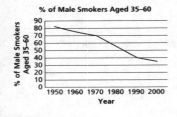

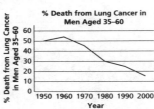

- While the two graphs on smoking (on page 24) cannot prove that lung cancer is caused by smoking, they do suggest that as the percentage of men smoking decreased, so too did deaths from lung cancer.
- It is, therefore, likely that the two variables are linked.

Use of Stem Cells in Medicine

- Stem cells are cells which can differentiate to become any cell type found in the body.
- They can be used to make new tissue and to replace tissues damaged by disease, e.g. to grow new nerve tissue to treat paralysis, or new heart valves to replace faulty ones.
- There are benefits and risks associated with using stem cells, as shown in the table below.

Potential Uses for Stem Cells

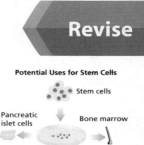

Benefits	Risks
Personal benefits to the person undergoing treatment	The stem cells may form tumours in the patient so may worsen the disease
Benefits to society since the process will provide knowledge that could lead to better future treatments	Stem cells may be rejected by the patient, which could lead to organ failure
Stem cells can be used to test new drugs	

- There are many ethical issues associated with using stem cells, e.g. some say that the use of stem cells sourced from human embryos is unethical and violates human rights as the embryos have 'no choice'.

Use of Gene Technology in Medicine

- Gene technology could be used in medicine to replace faulty genes, offering a cure for inherited conditions such as cystic fibrosis or diabetes.
- Replacing a faulty gene in the body has proved difficult to do.
- A virus is used to deliver the new gene and there are risks that the virus could harm the patient or deliver the gene to the wrong cell.

The Human Genome

- Genes can affect our chances of getting certain diseases.
- By studying the human genome, scientists hope to be able to predict the likelihood of a person getting a particular disease.
- Preventative action can then be taken.
- This is an example of personalised medicine.

Key Point

Some people are worried about the speed of developments in gene therapy, and are concerned that society does not fully understand the implications of these developments.

 Quick Test

1. How does diet impact on cardiovascular disease?
2. What is cancer?
3. What are the **three** options for treatment of cardiovascular disease?
4. Give **one** risk of using stem cell technology in medicine.

Key Words

cardiovascular
statin
stent

Genes

1 Corey describes himself to his friend.

For each feature, state whether it is caused by **genetics**, the **environment** or a **combination** of both.

a) 1.6 metres tall [1]

b) Blue eyes [1]

c) Pierced eyebrow [1]

d) Weight 90kg [1]

e) Scar on left cheek [1]

2 The diagrams below shows the distribution of blood groups in the United Kingdom and Asia.

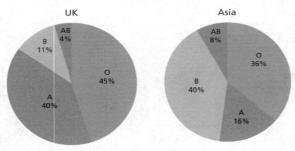

The table below contains data about the distribution of blood groups in Africa.

Group	% Population
O	50
A	25
B	21
AB	4

Draw a pie chart to show the distribution of blood groups in Africa. [3]

3 Sickle cell anaemia is a serious inherited blood disorder. The red blood cells, which carry oxygen around the body, develop abnormally.
It is caused by a recessive gene and a person with sickle cell anaemia must have two recessive alleles.

Use the letters **A** = no sickle cell anaemia and **a** = sickle cell anaemia.

a) What would be the phenotype of someone with the following alleles?

    i) AA [1]

    ii) Aa [1]

    iii) aa [1]

b) What would be the genotype of someone who was a carrier of sickle cell anaemia? [1]

4 Lesley was studying variation within her class.
She collected information on her friends' height, weight, eye colour, shoe size and whether they had freckles.

a) Divide the list above into continuous and discontinuous variations. [5]

b) Lesley plotted a bar chart of her results for shoe size.

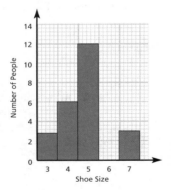

    i) Seven people in Lesley's class wear a size 6 shoe. Plot this information on the chart. [1]

    ii) Suggest how many people in Lesley's class might wear size 8 shoes. [1]

Total Marks _____ / 19

Review Questions

Genetics and Reproduction

1 What is the name of the type of cell division that leads to the formation of gametes? [1]

2 In humans, brown eyes is the dominant trait and blue eyes is the recessive trait.

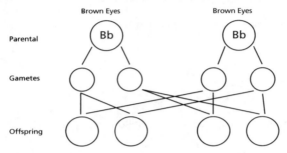

a) Complete the genetic cross above. [2]

b) Are the parents homozygous or heterozygous for eye colour? [1]

c) What is the ratio of brown eyes to blue eyes in the offspring? [1]

d) HT Each person's DNA base sequence differs slightly from other people's which gives rise to genetic variants.

   Explain how the change in base sequence could affect protein function. [3]

e) Circle the correct option in the sentence below.

   If both parents had blue eyes, there would be a **0% / 25% / 50% / 75% / 100%** chance that their offspring will have blue eyes. [1]

> **Total Marks** _____ / 9

Natural Selection and Evolution

1 In 1753, Carl Linnaeus classified the grey wolf as *Canis lupus,* the domestic dog as *Canis canis* and the coyote as *Canis latrans.*

In 1993, analysis of mitochondrial DNA from all three animals showed:

• the grey wolf and domestic dog share 99.8% of their DNA

• the grey wolf and coyote share 96% of their DNA.

Following this discovery, the domestic dog was reclassified as *Canis lupus familiaris.*

a) Which of the words below describes the word *'Canis'*.
Put a tick (✓) in the box next to the correct option.

Family	
Genus	
Species	

[1]

b) Suggest why the domestic dog was reclassified. [1]

c) Apart from results of DNA sequencing, suggest **one** other reason why organisms may need to be reclassified. [1]

d) There are many species of dogs.

What is meant by the word 'species'? [1]

2 People who have sickle cell anaemia are resistant to the tropical disease, malaria.
People with blood group O are more resistant to malaria than people with blood group A.
Malaria is more common in Africa than the United Kingdom.

Using Darwin's theory of natural selection, suggest why there is a larger percentage of people with blood group O in Africa than in the UK. [4]

3 Sometimes a mutation happens in a cell's DNA.

What is a mutation? [1]

Total Marks _____ / 9

Practice Questions

Monitoring and Maintaining the Environment

1. Some students wanted to survey the variety of organisms in an area by a canal.

   Draw a line from each survey to the best piece of apparatus for the students to use.

Survey	Apparatus
The variety of water invertebrates in the canal	Quadrat
The variety of plants growing by the side of the canal	Pitfall trap
The variety of flying insects in the long grass by the side of the canal	Sweep net
The variety of invertebrates found under the hedges along the side of the canal	Pond net

   [3]

2. Some students used the capture–mark–recapture method to estimate the number of slugs in a garden.
   In their first sample they caught 12 slugs, which they marked.
   In their second sample, which was collected a few days later, there were 10 slugs of which four were marked.

   What is the estimated population size of slugs in the garden? Show your working. [2]

3. Farmers **A** and **B** both grow carrots.
   Farmer **A** uses insecticides on his carrots.
   Farmer **B** does not.

   a) How will the use of insecticides benefit Farmer **A**? [1]

   b) Both farmers sell their carrots at the local market:

      Farmer **A**: fresh carrots 20p per kilogram

      Farmer **B**: fresh organic carrots 25p per kilogram.

      Why might some people be prepared to pay extra for Farmer **B**'s carrots? [1]

   c) The local conservation group are concerned that the number of farmland birds is decreasing.

      Explain how the use of insecticides could be contributing to this decrease. [2]

   Total Marks _____ / 9

Investigations

1 Look at the diagram of a pea, before and after germination.

If provided with water and a suitable temperature, germination should take about three days.

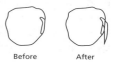

Before   After

A group of students want to find out the optimum temperature for germination of the pea.

Describe an investigation the students could do. Your description should include how to ensure the investigation is a fair test. [5]

> Total Marks _____ / 5

Feeding the Human Race

1 Explain how each of the following help meet the growing demand for food:

a) Using fertilisers [1]

b) Hydroponics [1]

2 HT Below are the stages of genetically engineering cabbages to produce a toxin that harms insects.
The toxin is produced naturally by bacteria.

    A   The gene is pasted into the DNA of a cabbage at an early stage of development.
    B   The gene for toxin production is cut out of the DNA.
    C   A strand of DNA is isolated from the bacteria.

a) Put the stages in the correct order. [1]

b) What is the name of the enzymes used in stages **A** and **B**? [2]

3 Look at the following food chain:

| Vegetables | ⟶ | Corn borer beetle | ⟶ | Chinese wasp |

Suggest how biological control could be used to improve the yield of vegetables. [2]

4 The following statements are about selectively breeding cows that produce good quantities of meat. They are not in the correct order.

A Offspring that produce a lot of meat are chosen.
B A cow and a bull which provide good quantities of meat are chosen as the parents.
C The offspring are bred together.
D The process is repeated over many generations.
E The parents are bred with each other.

Put the statements in the correct order. [1]

5 HT Scientists want to genetically engineer bacteria to produce proteins that can be used in vaccinations.
The gene for protein production is first isolated and cut from the donor DNA.
It is then inserted into a plasmid.

a) How is the gene for protein production cut from the donor DNA? [1]

b) Often, a marker gene for antibiotic resistance is also inserted into the plasmid.

What is the function of the marker gene? [1]

c) The plasmids with the new genes are mixed with the bacteria.
Not all bacteria will take up the plasmid.

How do scientists isolate the bacteria that have taken up the plasmid? [2]

d) The bacteria that have taken up the plasmid are put in a fermenter to reproduce.

Name **three** conditions that must be controlled in the fermenter. [3]

6 HT Scientists often use plasmids in genetic engineering.

a) What is a plasmid? [1]

b) Why do scientists use plasmids in genetic engineering? [1]

Total Marks _____ / 17

Monitoring and Maintaining Health

1 Draw a line from each disease to the method by which it is spread.

Disease	Method of Spread
Malaria	Contact
Cholera	By air
Tuberculosis	By water
Athlete's foot	Animal vector

[3]

2 The following paragraph is about tuberculosis.

Choose the correct word from each pair to complete the sentences.

Tuberculosis (TB) is a disease that affects the **lungs / liver**. People who have **HIV / cancer**

are more likely to catch TB because their **circulatory / immune** system is already weakened. [3]

3 Which of the following statements about HIV and AIDS are **true**? *

A AIDS is caused by HIV.
B AIDS can be cured if diagnosed early.
C The HIV virus can be treated with antivirals to prolong life expectancy.
D The virus can be spread by droplets in the air. [2]

4 White blood cells recognise antigens on the surface of
microorganisms and produce antibodies to attack them.

a) Look at the diagram. Which letter corresponds
to **i)** the microorganism, **ii)** the antigen and **iii)** the antibody? [2]

b) What is the name of the white blood cell that produces antibodies?
Circle the correct answer.

phagocyte   **lymphocyte**   **blastocyte** [1]

5 How do each of the following help to prevent the spread of plant disease?

a) Spraying plants with insecticides. [2]

b) Plants have cell walls and a waxy epidermis. [1]

c) HT Using DNA analysis. [2]

Total Marks _____ / 16

Prevention and Treatment of Disease

1 HT The following statements describe the stages in the production of monoclonal antibodies which bind to the hormone HCG.
They are in the wrong order.

A	Lymphocytes are fused with tumour cells.
B	A mouse is injected with the hormone HCG.
C	The monoclonal antibodies produced are collected.
D	Lymphocytes are collected from the mouse.
E	Hybridoma cells are grown in tissue culture.

a) Put the stages in the correct order. [2]

b) Suggest what these monoclonal antibodies could be used for. [1]

c) Give **one** other use of monoclonal antibodies. [1]

2 When working with microorganisms, it is important to use aseptic techniques.

Suggest **two** reasons why it is important to use aseptic techniques. [2]

3 Dakota goes to the doctors because she has a sore throat.
The doctor does **not** give her antibiotics.

Suggest why. [2]

4 Paul goes to the doctor with earache.
The doctor prescribes antibiotics and tells Paul that he must be sure to finish the course even if he feels better.

a) What type of organism may be responsible for Paul's earache? [1]

b) Why did the doctor tell Paul to finish the course even if he is feeling better? [2]

5 Put the stages below, about developing new medicines, in order. [3]

A	Tests on animals
B	Tests on healthy volunteers
C	Clinical trials
D	Tests on computer models or cells grown in the laboratory

6 Explain why it is important to test new drugs before they are released to the public. [3]

7 In the early 1800s, a doctor called Semmelweiss suggested that 'something' on the hands
of doctors and surgeons caused infections and could be spread from patient to patient.
By insisting that doctors washed their hands, he reduced patient deaths on hospital
wards from 12% to 1%.

a) What was the 'something' on the hands of doctors and surgeons? [1]

b) In modern hospitals, staff, patients and visitors are encouraged to wash their hands regularly.

   i) What type of substance is used in hand wash in hospitals? [1]

   ii) Suggest **one** precaution, other than hand washing, that surgeons take to reduce the
       spread of infection. [1]

Total Marks _____ / 20

Non-Communicable Diseases

1 Beatrice has been told that her arteries are coated with fatty deposits and that her cholesterol
levels are above normal.
The doctor wants to treat her with a drug to reduce her cholesterol levels.
The doctor tells her she may need an operation to make her arteries wider.

a) Suggest what drug the doctor may want to prescribe. [1]

b) What could be placed inside Beatrice's arteries to make them wider? [1]

2 Many lifestyle factors influence how likely it is that someone will suffer from certain diseases.

Explain the link between diet and heart disease. [3]

3 Ben goes to the doctor for an annual check up.
He drinks about 30 units of alcohol a week and is considerably overweight.
The doctor takes Ben's blood pressure and finds it is high.

What advice should the doctor give Ben? [4]

4 What are **two** conditions for which obesity is a risk factor? [2]

5 Which of the following statements best describes cancer? [1]

   A Cells begin to grow in the wrong place.
   B Cells become infected with cancer chemicals.
   C Cells begin to grow and divide uncontrollably.

Total Marks _____ / 12

Review Questions

Monitoring and Maintaining the Environment

1 Which of the sentences below best describes 'biodiversity'?
Put a tick (✓) in the box next your answer.

The variety among living organisms and the ecosystems in which they live	
The variety of habitats in an ecosystem	
A population within a community of organisms	

[1]

2 Explain how each of the following reduces biodiversity:

a) Deforestation [1]

b) Insecticide use [2]

3 Give **two** reasons why maintaining biodiversity is important. [2]

4 Neonicotinoid pesticides are new nicotine-like chemicals that act on the nervous systems of insects. They do not affect the nervous system of mammals like some previous pesticides.

These pesticides are water soluble, which means they can be applied to the soil and taken up by the whole plant, which then becomes toxic to any insects that try to eat it.

Neonicotinoids are often applied as seed treatments, which means coating the seeds before planting.

Dutch scientists are concerned that their use is responsible for the decline in the numbers of swallows, starlings and thrushes over the past 10 years.

The scientists have linked decreasing numbers of birds to areas where there are high levels of neonicotinoids in the surface water on fields.

The pesticide can remain in some soil types for up to three years.

a) Suggest **one** advantage and **one** disadvantage of the pesticide being water soluble. [2]

b) Why are neonicotinoids less harmful than some previous pesticides? [1]

c) Scientists have data to link decreasing bird numbers with pesticide levels, but they have yet to discover how the pesticide is causing this decrease.

Suggest **two** possible ways in which the pesticide could be responsible for decreasing bird numbers. [2]

d) The table below shows some data on bird numbers.

Average Concentration of Neonicotinoid in Surface Water in ng/ml	0	10	20	30
Number of Visiting Birds	12 000	11 988	11 650	11 600

Calculate the percentage decrease in the bird population when levels of neonicotinoids reach 30ng/ml.
Show your working and give your answer to two decimal places. [2]

Total Marks .... / 13

Investigations

1. Some students wanted to investigate the distribution of the meadow buttercup plant in the area around a local river. They had read that the meadow buttercup prefers damp areas to dry areas.

The equipment they used is shown below.

Tape measure   Quadrat   Moisture meter

The students' hypothesis was: 'Meadow buttercups prefer damp areas to dry areas'.

a) Describe how the students could use the equipment to test their hypothesis.
In your answer you should make reference to how each piece of equipment would be used. [5]

b) Another group of students were investigating the distribution of water snails in the river.
They used a pond net to sweep through the water and counted the number of snails in the net.
They did this 10 times in total before repeating the investigation further upstream.
Their results are shown below.

	Number of Snails in the Net at Each Sweep									
Downstream	3	6	5	4	6	2	2	3	4	4
Upstream	6	1	8	7	10	8	7	6	9	9

i) Calculate the mean, mode and median number of snails in one sweep of the downstream sample. [3]

Review Questions

ii) Which is the anomalous result in the upstream data? [1]

iii) Suggest **two** reasons for this anomalous result. [2]

Total Marks _____ / 11

Feeding the Human Race

1. The graph below shows the number of hectares used globally for genetically modified (GM) crops since 1998.

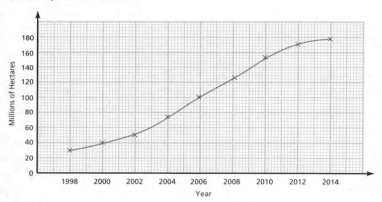

a) What are genetically modified crops? [1]

b) Between which years was there the highest increase in the use of land for GM crops? [1]

c) What percentage increase was there in use of land for GM crops between 1998 and 2014? Show your working. [2]

d) Give **two** reasons why scientists may want to genetically modify crop plants. [2]

2. Which of the following is an example of genetic engineering?
Put a tick (✓) in the box next to the true statement.

Placing a gene in barley plants to make them drought resistant	
Treating wheat with hormones to make a dwarf variety	
Taking the pollen from one type of lily and using it to pollinate a different type of lily with the hope of creating a new variety	

[1]

3 HT Genetic engineering can be used to produce rice which contains genes to combat
vitamin A deficiency.
These genes originally come from maize.

Explain how enzymes would be used in the transfer of genes from the maize to the rice. [4]

Total Marks _____ / 11

Monitoring and Maintaining Health

1 Use the diseases listed below to answer the questions.

malaria   **flu**   **athlete's foot**   **tuberculosis**

a) Which disease is caused by a fungus? [1]

b) Which disease is caused by a virus? [1]

c) Which disease would be treated with antibiotics? [1]

2 The diagram below shows one way in which the body deals with invading microorganisms.

a) What is the name of this process? [1]

b) What type of cell is involved in this process? [1]

3 The human body has a number of mechanisms to prevent microorganisms from gaining entry.

Describe how each of the following helps to defend the body.

a) Platelets [2]

b) Mucous membranes in the respiratory system [1]

Review Questions

4 Our white blood cells produce antibodies when foreign microorganisms invade our bodies.

Use the diagram below to explain why antibodies produced in response to the TB bacterium will **not** protect us against cholera.

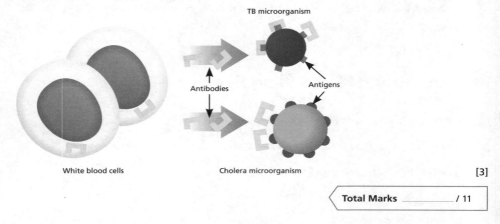

TB microorganism

Antibodies

Antigens

White blood cells

Cholera microorganism

[3]

Total Marks _____ / 11

Prevention and Treatment of Disease

1 HT When producing monoclonal antibodies, B lymphocytes are fused with tumour cells.

a) Which of the following is a reason for using tumour cells?
Put a tick (✓) in the box next to the correct answer.

They divide and grow rapidly	
They do not have a nucleus so there is more space for antibody production	
They are easy to detect	

[1]

b) What is the name of the cell produced from the fusion? [1]

2 Tanya and Charlie are best friends.
Tanya has been immunised against measles, but Charlie has not.
They come into contact with someone who has measles.
Charlie catches measles, but Tanya does not.

a) What was in the measles vaccine that Tanya was given? [1]

b) Explain why Tanya does **not** catch measles, but Charlie does. [3]

c) How is measles spread from one person to another? [1]

d) Charlie goes to the doctor. The doctor advises plenty of rest and painkillers if necessary.

Why does the doctor **not** prescribe antibiotics for Charlie? [2]

3 When new drugs are developed in the laboratory they are eventually tested in clinical trials.

State **two** ways that drugs are tested before clinical trials. [2]

4 In clinical trials, a control group of patients are often given a placebo.

What is the purpose of the control group? [1]

Total Marks _____ / 12

Non-Communicable Diseases

1 The table below shows how the percentage of adults with obesity in the United States changed over a 50-year period.

Year	1962	1974	1980	1994	2002	2008	2012
% Adults with Obesity	13	13	15	23	31	35	36

a) Plot a line graph of these results. [3]

b) Use the graph to predict what the percentage of people with obesity will be in 2015. [1]

c) Name **two** diseases that people with obesity are more likely to suffer from than people of normal weight. [2]

Total Marks _____ / 6

Answers

Page 5 Quick Test

1. An organism's complete set of DNA, including all of its genes
2. A capital letter shows a dominant allele; a lower case letter shows a recessive allele
3. **Any two from:** height; weight; skin colour; intelligence (Accept any other sensible answer)
4. a) **Any one from:** height; weight (Accept any other sensible answer)
   b) **Any one from:** blood group; right or left handed; shoe size (Accept any other sensible answer)

Page 7 Quick Test

1. Haploid cells have half the number of chromosomes found in a diploid cell, as they have just one copy of each chromosome, e.g. sperm or egg cell; diploid cells have two copies of each chromosome, e.g. normal body cell
2. Sexual reproduction involves two parents; involves the fusion of gametes; and the offspring are genetically different to their parents / asexual reproduction involves one parent; no gametes and the offspring are genetically identical to the parent
3. Eggs will always carry an X chromosome; sperm cells may carry an X or a Y chromosome; there is a 50% chance that an egg will fuse with a sperm carrying an X chromosome = XX (female); and there is a 50% chance that an egg will fuse with a sperm carrying a Y chromosome = XY (male)

Page 9 Quick Test

1. There is natural variation within any population; organisms with characteristics best suited to the environment are likely to survive, breed and pass on their successful genes to the next generation; animals with poor characteristics less well suited to the environment are less likely to survive and breed

> Don't forget 'breed and pass on genes'. It is an easy way to get two marks.

2. A bacterium mutates to become resistant to the antibiotic that is being used; the antibiotic kills all the sensitive bacteria; the resistant bacteria multiply creating a population of antibiotic-resistant bacteria
3. Organisms that are found to have very similar DNA will share common ancestors

Page 10 Genes

1. cell, nucleus, chromosome, gene [1] (1 mark for three in the correct place)
2. **A** Blood group [1]; **D** Eye colour [1]
3. a) Dominant [1]
   b) Heterozygous [1]
   c) ee [1]
4. Non-coding DNA [1]

Page 11 Genetics and Reproduction

1. 23 + [1]; 23 [1]; = 46 [1]
2. a) Sexual [1]
   b) Sexual [1]
   c) Asexual [1]
   d) Sexual [1]
   e) Asexual [1]
   f) Asexual [1]
   g) Sexual [1]
3. 4 [1]
4. a) Male [1]
   b) Diploid [1]
   c) 36 [1]
5. a) 1 = FF [1]; 2 = Ff [1]; 3 = Ff [1]; 4 = ff [1]
   b) 2 and 3 [2]
   c) 4 [1]

Page 12 Natural Selection and Evolution

1. a) Organisms with an advantage will survive to breed and pass on their genes to offspring [1]
   b) A bacterium mutates to become resistant [1]; sensitive bacteria are killed by the antibiotic [1]; resistant bacteria multiply rapidly to form large population [1]
2. a) C and D [1]
   b) E and F [1]
   c) C and G [1]

Page 15 Quick Test

1. Increased biodiversity offers greater opportunity for medical discoveries; it boosts the economy; it ensures sustainability (ecosystems more likely to recover after a 'natural disaster')
2. a) **Any two from:** hunting; overfishing; deforestation; farming single crops
   b) **Any two from:** creating nature reserves; reforestation; sustainable fishing
3. Tourism that aims to reduce the negative impact of tourists on the environment

Page 17 Quick Test

1. Measurements should be repeated
2. A result that does not fit the pattern of the rest of the results
3. Errors that are made every time that may be due to faulty equipment
4. It checks the design of the experiment and the validity of the data

Page 19 Quick Test

1. All people having access to sufficient, safe, nutritious food
2. Using living organisms to control number of pests / using the natural enemies to control the pest
3. The genes may get into wild flowers or crops; they may harm the consumers; we don't know the long-term effects

Page 21 Quick Test

1. **Any four from:** bacteria; viruses; fungi; protoctista; parasites
2. **Any three from:** air; water; food; contact; animals
3. **Any three from:** use pesticides; spread plants out; rotate crops; spray crops with fungicide or bactericide

Page 23 Quick Test

1. A cell that has resulted from the fusion of a cancer cell and a lymphocyte
2. Pregnancy testing; diagnosing cancer; treating cancer
3. White blood cells recognise the antigens on the dead or weakened pathogen that is in the vaccination. They make antibodies but also form memory cells. In a subsequent infection, memory cells produce antibodies quickly and in large numbers.

> Antibodies are produced **rapidly** and in **large numbers** in subsequent infections. These two words may gain you two marks.

4. Antibiotics act on bacteria; antivirals act on viruses; antiseptics are used on skin and surfaces to kill microorganisms

Page 25 Quick Test

1. Too much carbohydrate / fat can lead to obesity, which leads to high blood pressure and cardiovascular disease; a high fat diet can lead to increased levels of cholesterol, which coats the smooth lining of the arteries, causing them to narrow restricting blood flow and leading to heart attacks or strokes and high blood pressure; a diet high in salt can lead to high blood pressure.

> Remember, cholesterol coats **arteries** not veins.

2. Cancer is when cells grow and divide uncontrollably
3. Change in lifestyle; medication; surgery
4. Stem cells may develop into tumours / may be rejected by the patient

Page 26 Genes

1. a) Combination [1]
    b) Genetics [1]
    c) Environment [1]
    d) Combination [1]
    e) Environment [1]
2. A pie chart with four correctly drawn segments [3] (2 marks for two correct sections; 1 mark for one correct segment)

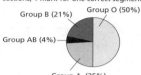

Group O (50%)
Group B (21%)
Group AB (4%)
Group A (25%)

3. a) i) No sickle cell anaemia [1]
        ii) No sickle cell anaemia but a carrier [1]
        iii) Sickle cell anaemia sufferer [1]
    b) Aa [1]
4. a) Continuous: height [1]; weight [1]
        Discontinuous: eye colour [1]; shoe size [1]; freckles [1]
    b) i) Bar correctly plotted to show 7 people [1]
        ii) **Accept**: 0, 1 or 2 [1]

Page 28 Genetics and Reproduction

1. Meiosis [1]
2. a) Correct gametes [1]; correct offspring [1]

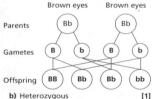

Brown eyes   Brown eyes
Parents   Bb   Bb
Gametes   B   b   B   b
Offspring   BB   Bb   Bb   bb

b) Heterozygous [1]
    c) Three brown : one blue / 3 : 1 [1]

> Ratios can be expressed in a number of ways: 3:1, 75%:25%, 0.75:0.25

d) The sequence of bases codes for amino acids [1]; the sequence of amino acids determines the protein made [1]; the protein made may not function correctly [1]
    e) 100% [1]

Page 29 Natural Selection and Evolution

1. a) Genus [1]
    b) New DNA evidence shows it to be very closely related to grey wolf [1]
    c) New fossils discovered [1]
    d) A group of similar animals that can breed to produce fertile offspring [1]
2. In Africa, people with blood group O

are resistant to malaria so they survive [1]; reproduce [1]; and pass on the O blood group to their offspring [1]; people with other blood groups are more likely to die from malaria [1]
3. A change in the sequence of bases in the DNA [1]

Page 30 Monitoring and Maintaining the Environment

1. Four correctly drawn lines [3] (2 marks for two correct lines; 1 mark for one)
    The variety of water invertebrates in the canal – Pond net
    The variety of plants growing by the side of the canal – Quadrat
    The variety of flying insects in the long grass by the side of the canal – Sweep net
    The variety of invertebrates found under the hedges along the side of the canal – Pitfall trap
2. $\frac{12 \times 10}{4}$ [1]; = 30 [1]
3. a) Farmer A will get a higher yield because less of the crop is lost to insect damage [1]
    b) People feel they are healthier / safer / better for the environment [1]
    c) They kill insects, which are the birds' food supply [1]; they poison birds [1]; and they damage eggs or young through accumulation in food chain [1]

Page 31 Investigations

1. **Answer must have:**
    Suitable number / range of temperatures (minimum of 3 temperatures at between 20 and 50°C) [1]
    Suitable number of peas used at each temperature (minimum 5) [1]
    Suitable time period to leave peas (2–3 days) [1]
    Simple method (must include adding water) [1]
    At least **two** other controlled variables (amount of water / size of peas / type of peas / amount of light / same growth medium, e.g. soil or cotton wool) [1]

Page 31 Feeding the Human Race

1. a) Fertilisers increase crop yield [1]
    b) Plants can be grown at all times of the year in an easily controlled environment [1]
2. a) C, B, A
    b) A = ligase enzyme [1]; B = restriction enzyme [1]
3. Introduce some Chinese wasps to the area [1]; since these will eat the corn borers [1]
4. B, E, A, C, D
5. a) Using restriction enzymes [1]
    b) Can be used to determine which bacteria take up the plasmid [1]
    c) Bacteria are grown on medium containing the antibiotic that the

marker is for [1]; only those with plasmid will be able to grow [1]
    d) Oxygen levels [1]; pH [1]; temperature [1]
6. a) Loop / ring of DNA [1]
    b) Plasmids can be inserted into bacteria and will replicate each time the bacteria divides [1]

Page 33 Monitoring and Maintaining Health

1. Four correctly drawn lines [3] (2 marks for two correct lines; 1 mark for one)
    Malaria – Animal vector
    Cholera – By water
    Tuberculosis – By air
    Athlete's foot – Contact
2. lungs [1]; HIV [1]; immune [1]
3. **A** AIDS is caused by HIV [1]; **C** The HIV virus can be treated with antivirals to prolong life expectancy [1]

> Do not confuse AIDS and HIV. HIV is the name of the virus. AIDS is the disease it causes.

4. a) A = microorganism, B = antibody, C = antigen [2] (1 mark for one correct)
    b) lymphocyte [1]
5. a) Insects can damage plants allowing microorganisms to enter [1]; insects can spread diseases from one plant to another [1]
    b) These provide a barrier to plant pathogens entering [1]
    c) By looking to see if there is DNA of plant pathogens [1]; present in the diseased plant tissue [1]

Page 34 Prevention and Treatment of Disease

1. a) B, D, A, E, C [2] (1 mark for three in correct place)
    b) Pregnancy testing [1]
    c) Detecting cancer / treating cancer [1]
2. Stop unwanted microorganisms contaminating cultures [1]; prevent microorganisms contaminating the surrounding area [1]
3. a) The sore throat is not caused by a bacterial infection / is caused by a virus [1]; antibiotics only kill bacteria [1]
4. a) Bacteria [1]
    b) Because there will still be microorganisms present even when he is feeling better [1]; without antibiotics these could start to multiply again, or even mutate into resistant strains [1]
5. D, A, B, C [3] (2 marks for two in correct places; 1 mark for one)
6. To test for efficacy / efficiency [1]; toxicity / safety [1]; dosage [1]
7. a) Bacteria / microorganisms [1]
    b) i) Antiseptic [1]
        ii) **Any one from:** gloves [1]; masks [1]; gowns [1]; all equipment sterilised [1]

Answers

Page 35 Non-Communicable Diseases

1. a) Statins **[1]**
   b) A stent **[1]**
2. High fat diet can lead to high cholesterol **[1]**; which narrows arteries **[1]**; causing high blood pressure, which puts a strain on heart **[1] OR** high salt intake **[1]**; causes high blood pressure **[1]**; which puts a strain on heart **[1] OR** eating more kJ energy / calories than used **[1]** leads to obesity **[1]**; which causes cardiovascular disease **[1]**
3. **Any four from:** drink less alcohol **[1]**; eat less **[1]**; lower salt intake **[1]**; switch to low fat products **[1]**; exercise more **[1]**
4. **Any two from:** Type 2 diabetes **[1]**; joint problems **[1]**; heart disease **[1]**; high blood pressure **[1]**; high cholesterol **[1]**
5. C Cells begin to grow and divide uncontrollably. **[1]**

Pages 36–41 Review Questions

Page 36 Monitoring and Maintaining the Environment

1. The variety among living organisms and the ecosystems in which they live **[1]**
2. a) Destroys habitats **[1]**
   b) Kill insects **[1]**; disrupts food chains **[1]**
3. **Any two from:** may lead to new medicines **[1]**; cures for diseases **[1]**; better economy **[1]**; ensures sustainability **[1]**
4. a) Advantage: can be applied to soil and will be taken in by plants **[1]** Disadvantage: can be washed away into water courses, rivers, etc. and can get into animals that drink the water **[1]**
   b) They do not affect the nervous system of mammals **[1]**
   c) The birds are consuming the pesticide when they drink water and this is harming them **[1]**; the birds are starving because the pesticide is killing their food source **[1]**
   d) Decrease = 12000 – 11600 = 400 **[1]**;
   % decrease = $\frac{400}{12000} \times 100 = 3.33\%$ **[1]**

Page 37 Investigations

1. a) Use the tape measure to mark a transect line from the river outwards across the field **[1]**; at suitable intervals, place a quadrat **[1]**; count the number of meadow buttercups in the quadrant **[1]**; measure the moisture content of the soil using the moisture meter **[1]**; repeat the transect in different areas / repeat and calculate average **[1]**
   b) i) Mean = 39 ÷ 10 = 3.9 **[1]**; mode = 4 **[1]**; median = 4 **[1]**
   ii) 1 **[1]**
   iii) **Any two from:** chance **[1]**; error made in counting **[1]**; net swept at different level **[1]**; net swept in different direction / angle **[1]**

Page 38 Feeding the Human Race

1. a) Plants which have had their DNA changed, usually by addition of a useful gene from another organism **[1]**
   b) 2002 and 2010 **[1]**
   c) $\frac{180}{30} \times 100$ **[1]**; = 600% **[1]**
   d) **Any two from:** insecticide resistance **[1]**; drought resistance **[1]**; able to grow in salty water **[1]**; increased nutritional content; increased shelf life **[1]**
2. Placing a gene in barley plants to make them drought resistant **[1]**
3. Restriction enzyme **[1]**; to cut the gene from the maize plant DNA **[1]**; Ligase enzyme **[1]**; to paste the gene into rice plant DNA (or accept plasmid) **[1]**

Page 39 Monitoring and Maintaining Health

1. a) Athlete's foot **[1]**
   b) Flu **[1]**
   c) Tuberculosis **[1]**
2. a) Phagocytosis **[1]**

> Remember, the word **phagocytosis** means to devour the cell.

   b) A phagocyte **[1]**
3. a) Form a clot **[1]**; which seals the wound **[1]**
   b) Trap microorganisms and dirt **[1]**
4. The antibodies produced against the tuberculosis (TB) bacterium are designed to recognise and lock onto the antigens on its surface (or accept: specific to TB bacteria) **[1]**; the antigens on the cholera virus are different **[1]**; and the TB antibodies will not recognise them or fit onto them **[1]**

Page 40 Prevention and Treatment of Disease

1. a) They divide and grow rapidly **[1]**
   b) Hybridoma **[1]**
2. a) Dead / weakened measles virus **[1]**
   b) Tanya already had antibodies against the measles virus **[1]**; she also has memory cells **[1]**; which can quickly produce large numbers of antibodies **[1]**
   c) In the air / moisture droplets **[1]**
   d) Measles in caused by a virus **[1]**; antibiotics cannot be used for viral infections / can only be used for bacterial infections **[1]**
3. **Any two from:** tested on cells **[1]**; animals **[1]**; computer models **[1]**; healthy volunteers **[1]**
4. To compare the results of people taking the drug to those who have not taken the drug **[1]**

Page 41 Non-Communicable Diseases

1. a) Correctly labelled axes **[1]**; correctly plotted points **[1]**; joined by a smooth curve **[1]**

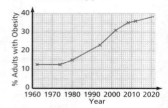

   b) 37% **[1]**
   c) **Any two from:** heart disease **[1]**; type 2 diabetes **[1]**; high blood pressure **[1]**; liver disease **[1]**

Notes

Notes